Original title:
The Ocean's Quiet Dance

Copyright © 2025 Creative Arts Management OÜ
All rights reserved.

Author: Rosalie Bradford
ISBN HARDBACK: 978-1-80587-372-3
ISBN PAPERBACK: 978-1-80587-842-1

Breath of the Deep Blue

The waves roll in, they giggle and play,
A fish in a tux, stealing the day.
Seagulls compete in a squawking race,
While crabs in the sand sport a silly face.

The sun dips low, it's time for a show,
A dolphin in shades puts on a flow.
Splashing around like he's king of the sea,
With a flip and a twist, oh look at me!

Surrender to Brooding Waters

The tide comes in with a wobbly glee,
A turtle who thinks he swims like a bee.
Jellyfish styling, with colors that clash,
While seashells giggle at the funny splash.

A crab with a hat prances on the shore,
Doing the cha-cha, but oh, what's in store?
He slips in the foam, what a comical view,
The seaweed just dances, saying, 'This one's for you!'

Harmony of the Seafoam

Bubbles are giggling, whispering spells,
A starfish telling tall tales, oh what a swell!
A whale with a grin plays peek-a-boo,
While sea cucumbers cheer, 'We see you too!'

Fish in a line, practicing their tango,
Each little wiggle, a colorful fandango.
The coral is clapping, it's quite the surprise,
As everyone joins in with big, happy sighs!

Ebbing into Stillness

The moonlight flickers, all creatures unite,
A clam's nightly gossip brings laughter so bright.
Octopus juggling, with each tentacle free,
While the waves sway gently, chuckling in glee.

A seal, wearing glasses, reads a fishy book,
Each page is a splash, with a twist and a hook.
As night settles down, and the sea takes a bow,
The tide whispers softly, 'Good night to you now!'

Weightless Whispers of the Abyss

In the deep where fish play hide,
A turtle sneezes, how absurd!
The bubbles giggle, side by side,
While jellyfish float, blissfully blurred.

A crab's new dance is quite a sight,
He's moonwalking past the reef.
Starfish cheer, oh what a night!
This deep-sea party is beyond belief!

Meditative Depths of the Lagoon

In a pond where frogs croak tunes,
And ducks wear hats of leafy green,
A splash from fish, they tease the moons,
Who knew the deep could be so keen?

The otter's juggling clams with flair,
While seahorses form a line,
They nod and laugh, without a care,
In this lagoon, all's simply divine!

Hidden Ballet of the Brine

With pirouettes, the fish do twirl,
Like tiny dancers dressed in scale,
A mermaid's hair is a swirly whirl,
She giggles as they spin, set sail.

A seagull swoops with a caw and flap,
Dropping snacks into the blue abyss,
But the crabs know it's all a trap,
At lunch, they promise not to miss!

Velvet Waves in Stillness

A seal in shades lounges with glee,
Waves tickle toes of unsuspecting birds,
Seashells play tag, just wait and see,
Who knew the sea had such quirky herds?

A fishy joke cannot be contained,
They laugh until the tide rolls in,
With every wave, new humor gained,
In this stillness, let the fun begin!

Silence in the Salted Air

A seagull squawks, then takes a dive,
Catching snacks as we all thrive.
The breeze can tickle, make us laugh,
While crabs might pinch, oh, what a gaffe!

We splash around, pretending to swim,
As waves try hard to make us dim.
Each splash a joke, a giggle shared,
In this salty realm, we're all kids, unprepared!

Dappled Light on the Water's Surface

Sunbeams frolic on rippled glass,
Fish make faces as they pass.
With every wave, a splash and plop,
A dance breaks out, we can't stop!

Little boats bob like they're at a show,
Each oar a comedian, putting on a glow.
Who knew that water could tickle so?
With each gentle wave, it steals the show!

Embrace of the Tranquil Tide

The tide comes in, a gentle tease,
Stealing shoes with playful ease.
Flip-flops fly, what a comical sight,
As laughter rolls with the waves' delight!

Shells whisper secrets, crabs play the clown,
Sandcastles wave their tiny crowns.
We dodge the water, but it won't retreat,
Laughter spills out, oh what a treat!

Shadows of Sirens in Slumber

Under the waves, they giggle and play,
Sirens dreaming, making anchors sway.
Their dreams of pranks in watery beds,
While we chase fish with silly threads!

The splash of fins, like sneezes in the sea,
A whale might wink, just for the spree.
In these depths, every ripple holds cheer,
Come join the fun, there's nothing to fear!

Languid Movements of the Water's Edge

Waves come in wearing a goofy grin,
They tickle toes like a playful kin.
Seagulls squawk, doing silly dives,
As shells gossip on sand, they thrive.

Crabs in tuxedos, shuffling about,
Moonwalking sideways, they twist and sprout.
The tide plays tag, with footprints in tow,
As sandcastles tremble, 'Oh no! Oh no!'

Starfish lounge like they own the place,
Sipping saltwater, sporting a face.
"Life's a beach!" they seem to declare,
While driftwood dances without a care.

Under the sun, the sea frolics free,
Bubbles rise up, just like you and me.
With laughter of waves, they splash and fling,
At the coast where the zany sea critters swing.

The Unseen Ballet of the Surf

Waves waltz in with a gentle bow,
But trip on rocks as they take a vow.
The fish that flirt, in a school parade,
Spin, twirl, and glide with a splash brigade.

Seashells whisper secrets to the sand,
Each crabs' dance is completely unplanned.
While turtles chuckle, moving so slow,
As jellyfish float like they're putting on a show.

The sun plays spotlight on frolicking fluke,
Fish flick their tails as if reading a book.
Underwater, a party begins to arise,
With seaweed swaying, it's the best surprise!

From dolphins' leaps to sea urchins' prance,
In this salty world, everyone gets to dance.
And as the tide turns, they gather 'round tight,
All in good fun, till the fall of the night.

Melodies of Hushed Waters

Water whispers secrets low,
A fish caught dancing to and fro.
Seagulls squawk, they tease the tide,
While crabs perform with utmost pride.

Shells are ears to gossip's tale,
A playful dolphin starts to wail.
Stars above in laughter gleam,
As seaweed sways on a silly dream.

Featherlight Currents at Dusk

The waves play tag with sandy feet,
While starfish grooves to a lively beat.
A hermit crab wears quite a crown,
As tides lift toys of seashells down.

Gull giggles echo, so off-key,
A dolphin winks, says, 'Come swim with me!'
The moon does a jig, round and round,
Chatting with the starfish lost and found.

Mystic Embrace of the Abyss

In depths where silliness won't drown,
Jellyfish twirl like clowns in town.
Sea cucumbers play hide and seek,
While narwhals sing in notes unique.

Octopuses share ghost stories tight,
Scaring all fish with frights at night.
Giant squids pull pranks with glee,
Their ink clouds form a jubilee.

Reveries on the Pacific Edge

Where the frothy waves do jig and hop,
Starfish laugh as they plop and flop.
Crabs wear sunglasses like beach bums do,
Waving hello to the buoys anew.

The breeze tells jokes that tickle the sea,
While barnacles grin with mirthful glee.
Sandcastles boast their sandy might,
Though a wave sneaks up to end the fight.

Feathered Waves and Starry Sky

Seagulls argue at sunset, oh what a sight,
They squawk and dive, giving fish a fright.
A crab wears a hat, all made of seaweed,
Strutting with flair, he's a real funny breed.

Waves giggle softly, tickling the sand,
While starfish laugh, forming a playful band.
Jellyfish jiggle, doing their best dance,
In a wobbly fashion, they twirl and prance.

Echoes of Calm in Turquoise Depths

The fish wear sunglasses, chilling in style,
Turtles swim by, giving the sea a smile.
A clam tells a joke, the shellfish do gleam,
As laughter bubbles up in this underwater dream.

Coral reefs echo with giggles and grins,
As octopuses juggle with colorful fins.
Anemones wave, their friends all in tow,
In this turquoise realm, hilarity flows.

Ethereal Dance of the Undercurrents

Mermaids giggle, brushing their long hair,
While dolphins flip flops without a care.
They dive and they dart, so full of delight,
Making waves of laughter that last through the night.

Urchins in costumes, they dance on the floor,
Sea cucumbers shuffle, but what's more,
They tell silly tales of what's past and what's new,
In an underwater party where everyone's blue.

Tales from the Tranquil Shore

A sandcastle prince, with a grainy crown,
Commands all the crabs to dance up and down.
Seashells cheer loudly, they love the parade,
As tide pools applaud, their laughter won't fade.

The sun sets in colors, a marvelous show,
While beach balls bounce where the giggling waves flow.
With ice cream in hand, they share silly fables,
Of clams with wild dreams and starfish in stables.

The Dance of Shimmering Shores

Seagulls strut like they've got flair,
While crabs scuttle with a salty glare.
Waves tickle toes in a playful tease,
Shells gossip softly, floating with ease.

Starfish snap their fingers in delight,
Jellyfish jiggle, glowing in the night.
Sandcastles wobble with royal fuss,
As the tide giggles and goes on a bus.

Subtle Movements of the Tide

The tide rolls in with a little splash,
Playing tag with the rocks in a flash.
Tiny fish dance in a circus show,
While dolphins giggle, putting on a glow.

Octopuses twirl with eight legs in sync,
One turns purple, others turn pink.
They wave at the folks who come to play,
And then sneak off, laughing all the way.

Murmuring Beneath the Surface

Bubbles pop like secrets in the sea,
Anemones sway, looking quite free.
Mermaids hum with a mischievous flair,
As seaweed waltzes without a care.

Clownfish giggle, darting to and fro,
While turtles roll slow, taking it slow.
Every coral dances in hues so bright,
Underwater parties last into the night.

Celestial Waves at Rest

Twinkling stars take a break on the shore,
As the waves whisper, "We've danced before!"
Sand crabs meditate, zen in the sun,
Sharing secrets of joy, just having fun.

The moon smiles down on the splashing play,
Inviting sea creatures to the ballet.
With each gentle ripple, they all take a chance,
In this sparkling night, they continue to dance.

Subtle Movements of the Tide

Waves tiptoe in a breezy waltz,
Seagulls squawk, they hold their pulse.
Fish wear hats, swim backwards with flair,
The sand grins wide, playing unfair.

Crabs start a conga, oh what a sight,
Dancing on toes, in the moonlight bright.
Jellyfish juggle, quite out of time,
While clams clap along, to a silent rhyme.

Starfish cheerleaders fluff their soft backs,
In a shell-boat parade, no one relax.
Waves giggle and tickle, what a tease,
As the seaweed sways, like it's got a disease.

Lighthouses spin in a swirling groove,
With lanterns that twinkle, they try to move.
A dolphin pops up, with a belly full of laughs,
While the moon winks down at our funny paths.

Veils of Mist over Waters

Misty veils dance, all soft and sly,
With foggy whispers, they pass by.
The boats wear pajamas, snoozing on waves,
While fish play poker, making bold braves.

Mermaids giggle, fixing their hair,
With shells and bubbles, floating in air.
A sea serpent ties up knots for fun,
While barnacles shout, "Come on, let's run!"

The otters tumble, in a swirling spree,
Pretending to be in a bumblebee.
Starfish throw shade, in a game of catch,
As krill stream by, all ready to hatch.

In the misty laughter, no worries arise,
The waves just giggle, with mischievous eyes.
As the sun peeks through, in a golden reply,
The sea takes a bow, with a heartfelt sigh.

The Stillness Between the Swells

In the calm between waves, a bubble pops,
And fish in tuxedos plop and flop.
Seashells gossip with giggles galore,
As turtles tiptoe, and dolphins roar.

The gulls wear glasses, reading the tides,
While starfish offer some whimsical guides.
A pelican tries a belly flop dive,
But misses the splash, it's a sure jive!

In the hush, whispers of seaweed sway,
Making jokes like they're on holiday.
With splashbacks and flips, they play 'who will win?'
While barnacles chuckle, delighted within.

Under this stillness, a party unfolds,
With laughter and joy that the ocean holds.
When swells finally rise, it's a wild ballet,
And even the sea foam can't help but sway!

Under the Gaze of the Stars

Stars blink down, like they're in a race,
As jellyfish glow, with a ghostly grace.
Octopuses tango, in the moon's bright beam,
While crabs play cards, plotting their scheme.

Shells snap jokes about waves that crash,
While sea cucumbers make quite the splash.
They murmur secrets, in bubbles of joy,
As fish play tag with a lively decoy.

The coral reefs giggle, in a vibrant array,
With colors that dance, like it's a cabaret.
Under starlight, the waters prance,
Every splash and ripple, a cheeky romance.

As the tide rolls back, and the night draws deep,
The ocean holds treasures, in silence and sleep.
But just like a comedian with one final jest,
It tickles our toes, it's still all for the best!

Dreamy Shores in Twilight

In twilight's glow, the seagulls strut,
Crabs wearing hats, oh what a nut!
Waves tickle toes with wobbly glee,
Shells whisper secrets, oh, come and see.

Footprints dance like they lost a race,
Starfish giggle, they can't keep pace.
Jellyfish waltz, but they trip and fall,
Sandcastles bow, they're the funniest of all.

Seashells play tunes, a jazzy scene,
While hermit crabs sport a snazzy sheen.
Tide pools chuckle, what a delight,
As seaweed joins for a funky night.

With every splash, the laughter grows,
Fish wear glasses, striking poses.
The sun sinks low, and what a show,
On dreamy shores, the fun won't slow!

Swaying with the Sea Breeze

Breezes tickle, oh the fun,
Kites are laughing, on the run.
Flip-flops dance to a silly beat,
While dolphins play tag, oh what a treat!

Seagulls squawk in a chatty spree,
Waves high-five, so joyfully.
Surfers tumble, eat some sand,
Saltwater gets in, oh isn't it grand?

Starfish giggle atop the rocks,
Waiting for crabs in their silly frocks.
Seashells whisper jokes, just for fun,
As waves paint smiles under the sun.

The lighthouse winks with playful light,
Guiding all giggles through the night.
With every gust, the world spins round,
In this breezy party, joy is found!

Ripples of Tranquility

In ripples soft, a frog takes a leap,
Wobbling in circles, it can't help but peep.
Goldfish wear hats, so stylish and bright,
As they plan a disco for Friday night.

The moon beams down, with a cheeky grin,
Creating a spotlight for fish to twirl in.
Crabs get groovy on the shoreline's edge,
As waves clap hands, forming a pledge.

A turtle glides, trying to vogue,
While seaweed flops in a funky rog.
Ripples giggle beneath the pale light,
Trusting the tide to keep spirits bright.

Driftwood sings with a raspy croon,
While bright shells dance, under the moon.
In tranquil waters, life's a spree,
With ripples of laughter, wild and free!

Shadows Among the Corals

In coral realms where shadows prance,
Eels poke noses for a silly glance.
Octopuses juggle, trying so hard,
While crabs play poker, tossing a card.

The fish throw parties, a glittery bash,
Where starfish twirl in a flashy splash.
Clownfish giggle, their jokes are great,
While the sea anemone sets up the plate.

As sea cucumbers glide with flair,
Whales join in, singing without a care.
Coral castles echo with joyous tunes,
Sending laughter to the light of the moons.

In shadows deep, the fun unfolds,
With playful secrets that the ocean holds.
Next time you're near, don't miss the chance,
To join in the rhythm of the ocean's dance!

Choreography of Pebbles and Foam

Pebbles giggle as they roll,
They take a break for a small stroll.
Foam does twirl and twist about,
Whispering secrets, no doubt!

Bubbles bounce in a silly way,
Playing hopscotch in the bay.
The tide hums a jolly tune,
While sandcastles shake to the moon.

Clams tap dance with their little feet,
As crabs join in with a cheeky beat.
Seagulls laugh and join the fun,
Under the bright and shining sun.

Watch the seaweed sway and sway,
In a comical game of ballet.
The ocean's jokes, a playful trance,
Oh, what a wacky, watery dance!

Calm Harbor of Whispers

In the harbor, boats spin 'round,
Making laughter, what a sound!
Tugs are winking at the shore,
While sails tell stories and more.

Fish are gossiping quite sly,
With bubbles rising, oh so high.
The dock is busy, what a sight,
As seagulls squawk with all their might.

A lighthouse beams with joyful grace,
Waving to ships with a smiling face.
Here laughter floats on little waves,
While sailors dance as the sunlight braves.

Crabs wear hats, looking so grand,
Pretending to rule this sandy land.
A calm harbor, full of cheer,
Where whispers giggle, loud and clear!

Twilight Waltz of the Tidal Line

The sun dips low, a golden prize,
The tide begins its sparkly rise.
Starfish pirouette in delight,
While dolphins leap into the night.

Moonbeams shimmer on the waves,
As sea otters gather in caves.
Shells make music, a light clink,
As jellyfish sway, and briefly blink.

Tide pools bubble in a jolly show,
With starry eyes, they steal the glow.
The evening breeze whispers along,
As crabs and clams hum a soft song.

Sand drifts by with a gentle hand,
Wishing for more dance on this land.
A twilight waltz on a watery floor,
Where laughter rings forevermore!

Windswept Serenity of the Surf

Waves tumble in with a playful grin,
Like puppies racing, trying to win.
Sand kicks up as they play tag,
As giggles echo from a flag.

Seagulls caw in a comical squawk,
Pointing out the rocks for a walk.
Surfboards laugh as they catch a wave,
Holding a party, merry and brave.

In the breeze, kites start to dance,
Making the clouds do a funny prance.
Chasing the sun, they weave and twirl,
A windswept dream in a salty whirl.

Coconut drinks, everyone cheers,
As the surf rolls in, spreading good vibes here.
Serenity meets a humorous flair,
An ocean of smiles floats in the air!

Serenade of the Sea

The fish wear tiny hats, so spry,
They waltz beneath the waves up high.
With crabs in shoes that make them prance,
They giggle while they take a chance.

A dolphin sings a silly tune,
While seaweed sways like it's in June.
The starfish claps its five small hands,
In this flowery, silly land.

Jellyfish float and bob around,
As clams just laugh without a sound.
The sharks skate by in roller shoes,
While turtles wear the latest blues.

So come, my friend, and join the fun,
Where sea creatures dance, and laughter's spun.
They've all agreed, this is the place,
To boogie in a watery space.

Gentle Currents of Serenity

A squid with shades slides by in style,
With jellybeans, it makes a pile.
Crabs play cards with funny looks,
While snails cram in their comic books.

The sea turtles race on tiny bikes,
While fish crack jokes that spark delights.
An octopus counts to ten and slips,
As dolphins spin with twirls and flips.

The coral shakes with giggles sweet,
As sea cucumbers groovy beat.
They toss some bubbles, big and wide,
And laugh until the tide takes pride.

So join this world with smiles abound,
Where silly friends are always found.
In gentle waves, there's glee to share,
Where laughter bubbles in salty air.

Moonlit Murmurs Above

On moonlit nights, the sea folks jam,
With stingrays strumming on a clam.
A porpoise hums a tune so bright,
While all the sea stars shine for light.

A crab MC spins tales of old,
While mermaids dance in gowns of gold.
With winks and nods, the octopuses,
Turn quiet tides to joyous fusses.

The sea floor shakes with laughter loud,
As fish parade, they're quite a crowd.
The water sparkles, full of glee,
In this silly, moonlit spree.

So grab a seat on the sandy shelf,
And join the fun; just be yourself.
Under the stars, the laughter clings,
In whispered joy, the ocean sings.

Fluid Rhythms of the Deep

In deep blue seas, the antics swell,
As submarines of fish do yell.
With costumes on for fashion shows,
The seaweed twirls with all it knows.

A crab in shades and flip-flops too,
Leads a parade of fish, it's true.
As seahorses line dance in pairs,
While everyone joins without any cares.

The sea anemones bow and sway,
As currents carry jokes away.
They roll and flip, a frothy spree,
In the watery world of wild glee.

With bubbles rising, laughter flows,
From friendly clams, to fish, it goes.
Join this madcap ocean tale,
Where happiness will always sail.

Whispered Stories of the Sea

A fish sat down with a shell,
To swap some tales and laugh as well.
They spoke of a crab with a big ol' hat,
And how he danced like a clumsy cat.

A jellyfish floated, feeling quite grand,
With tendrils that looked like they'd been planned.
He boasted of parties held in the foam,
Where mermaids and dolphins felt right at home.

A seagull, perched high on a rock,
Chimed in about his favorite dock.
He stated, with glee, he's a real cool bird,
Until he got chased by a clam—how absurd!

So next time you hear that soft ocean sound,
Remember the stories that giggle abound.
For underwater pals, with a wink and a grin,
Keep laughing and dancing, let the fun begin!

Enchanted Depths and Breezes

Bubbles giggle as they rise,
While sea turtles wear funny ties.
They glide with grace on their ocean ride,
While octopuses hide snacks inside.

A starfish twirled on a coral stage,
Singing sweet songs of the underwater age.
But oh, that crab, with his tap dance feet,
Tripped over sea urchins—what a treat!

A whale blew bubbles, quite the sight,
While a clownfish danced, feeling light.
But when a shark tried to join the fun,
He fumbled and tumbled—oh, what a run!

So hear the tales of the sea's delight,
Where laughter echoes both day and night.
Each wave a whisper of joy unfurled,
In these enchanted depths, the fun's around the world!

The Quiet Waltz of Nature's Flow

A crab and a shrimp in a waltz so sweet,
Tripped over sea weeds, now that's a feat!
They laughed and they tumbled across the sandy floor,
While starfish clapped—what a comical score!

The waves whispered secrets, soft and sly,
A dolphin jumped high, then waved goodbye.
With every splash and every twist,
The ocean was filled with a giggling mist.

A seahorse pranced with a twinkling grand,
He wore a bowtie, looking quite spanned.
But a crab pinched his tie in a wild jest,
Now that's fashion—talk about a pest!

Each ripple of water holds laughter and cheer,
As nature waltzes, bringing us near.
For in these currents, both silly and bright,
The joy of the sea is a wondrous sight!

Reflection on the Velvet Waves

The waves have secrets that bubble and pop,
From fish playing tag to a seaweed swap.
They whisper jokes with a splash and a glide,
While a crab tells tales, all full of pride.

A stingray glided by with a wink,
Expressing how he loves to rethink.
"Why do we schools? Just for some fun!"
But his buddy the flounder just said, "You've won!"

A dolphin surged forth with a silly dance,
Making fish giggle, they took a chance.
But who could have known, with a flip and a spin,
He'd land in a seaweed—what a chin-chin!

With every wave that rolls and sways,
Comes laughter echoed in playful ways.
So dive into the blue and let out a cheer,
For the velvet waves hold joy crystal clear!

Tranquil Depths of Blue

Bubbles rise in gentle cheer,
A fish performs its wiggly steer.
A clam just laughed, it's quite absurd,
It's hard to hear beneath the word!

Seaweed sways, a lonely dance,
With twirls and spins, it takes its chance.
The starfish claps with joy to see,
A crab do the cha-cha merrily!

Silken Swells at Dusk

Waves come in with giggling glee,
They tickle toes—oh, silly me!
A seagull swoops, it stole my fries,
With flappy wings, it waves goodbyes!

A dolphin jumps, it dares to play,
While fish in suits swim by the bay.
"Where's the party?" they all shout,
As jellyfish float and twist about!

Echoes of a Calm Horizon

The sun dips low, the sky's a game,
A pelican shouts, but who's to blame?
Shells wear hats, the sea is bright,
A sand crab grins, it feels polite!

Mermaids gossip, tails in a swirl,
While octopuses start to twirl.
"Oh, look at that!" they all exclaim,
As starfish show off in a name game!

Lullaby of the Salted Air

As night creeps in, the light grows soft,
The crabs play tag, but then they scoff!
A whale hums low, a funny tune,
While seahorses dance under the moon.

Tiny shrimp wear tiny shoes,
"Oh, what a sight!" they sing the blues.
With nets and laughs, they all unite,
In this bizarre but charming night!

Harmonies of the Briny Depths

In the deep where fishes play,
A crab clicks his claws, ballet!
Seaweed swings with gentle grace,
While jellyfish float in their pace.

Barnacles start a rock 'n' roll,
As octopuses lose control!
Turtles laugh at the fish's spin,
They say, 'Now let the games begin!'

Clams clap shells to the beat,
While seahorses sway on their feet.
A long-haired mermaid hums a tune,
As sleepy sharks nap, all too soon.

Starfish cheer on a crab's big leap,
As bubbles burst and oceans weep.
With flippers twirling round and round,
The briny depths are never bound!

The Dance of Still Waters

Ripples ripple without a care,
Ducks do ballet, unaware.
A frog leaps high to take the stage,
While fish applaud from their cage.

A snail in shades spins quite a tale,
As dragonflies start to flail.
The breeze whispers, 'You're in my way!'
Leaves join in for a light ballet.

The sun dips low to take a bow,
The moon thinks, 'What's happening now?'
Waves clap their hands in laughter wide,
As night makes all the fish slide!

Stars twinkle as a clam rhymes,
With crabs that dance to jokes and chimes.
And every splash brings endless glee,
In this still depth, wild and free!

Caress of the Coastal Night

The beach balls roll on the shore,
Where seagulls squawk and beg for more.
Sandcastles wobble, soon to fall,
As kids build towers, standing tall.

In the moonlight, crabs conspire,
Plotting mischief by the fire.
They wear hats and start a toast,
'Here's to the sea, our lively host!'

Laughter echoes, shells do chime,
The night dance feels truly sublime.
A dolphin leaps, then takes a bow,
While starfish cheer, 'You're the wow!'

With all the tides that ebb and flow,
Even the seaweed starts to glow.
Life's a party, come take a chance,
Join the fun, let your heart prance!

Folklore of the Marine Serenade

Whispers of fish fill the tide,
With tales of mermaids that once tried.
They danced with dolphins, laughed with glee,
In a conga line, full and free!

A pufferfish tried to tell a joke,
But he burst out laughing, what a poke!
'I'm full of air, and yet so spry,
Why did the seaweed wave goodbye?'

An eel just chuckled, what a sight,
'It's all in fun in the pale moonlight!'
So they swirl and spin with delight,
Making memories, holding tight.

The waves join in with playful sounds,
Echoing through the salty grounds.
Underneath the stars' bright glow,
The ocean's tunes will always flow!

Ephemeral Dances on the Beach

Waves waltz in a goofy line,
They tiptoe, splash and then recline.
Seagulls laugh with flapping wings,
Watching as the shoreline sings.

Footprints vanish, the tide's a prank,
Ocean tickles, we all just flank.
Sandcastles tumble, with a puff,
The seaside's giggle is quite enough.

Starfish posing, such a sight,
Trying to dance, but it's not quite right.
Crabs in tuxedos, scuttle and jive,
Each wave's visit feels alive!

Shells gossip tales from afar,
Whispering secrets, bizarre bazaar.
As bubbles pop with cheerful sounds,
Joy in splashes, laughter abounds.

Soft Secrets of the Coastal Sands

Sands wear silly hats of brown,
Turtles chuckle, won't let you frown.
The dunes keep secrets, oh so sly,
While flip-flops dance, oh me, oh my!

Crabs in disco, moving fast,
They groove to tunes that never last.
Seashells giggle in a line,
With salty winds, they feel divine.

The beach asks softly, where's your shoe?
And pupfish spin a tricky view.
Dolphins leap, but one will fall,
In this vast, silly water ball.

With laughter echoing every wave,
The sandy world, a playful cave.
Moments shimmer on sunny days,
In the soft sands where funny plays.

The Quietude of Brackish Waters

Where whispers mingle with the tides,
Fish throw parties, no one hides.
They swirl like dancers wearing scales,
In brackish muck, it never fails.

Frogs hold concerts, sing their best,
While turtles nap, they take a rest.
The reeds sway gently, shaking hands,
To tease the mud and play in bands.

Crabs equipped with tiny hats,
Join the jams and tease the rats.
A heron's stance, in deep thought,
Looks rather silly, just like it ought.

With soft splashes, they take a bow,
Water's secrets—whisper now!
The quiet's packed with quirky fun,
Brackish laughter, never done.

Subdued Harmony of the Horizon

The sky blushes with a cheeky grin,
As waves tickle toes, come on in!
Horizon dips with a playful wink,
Fish find bubbles, don't you think?

The sun dips low, can't seem to stay,
Brushing clouds in a funny way.
And starfish giggle on their beds,
Poking at seagulls, using heads.

Waves strut by, they've got a beat,
Sending foam to tickle your feet.
Each splash is bursting with delight,
Dancing shadows greet the night.

In the calm, the silliness flows,
Where laughter lives, the horizon glows.
All around, the world's a jest,
As waves moonwalk, they surely jest.

Timeless Swell of the Sea

Waves in tuxedos, do a jump,
They flip and flounder, make a thump.
Seagulls chuckle, join the show,
"Look at us!" they squawk, and go.

Crabs wear bow ties, strutting proud,
While fish practice, swimming loud.
The starfish laugh, weirder still,
As they twirl round, chasing shrill.

Clams are judges, very stern,
Counting points for each cool turn.
When the tide rolls out for a snooze,
They all just giggle, sharing news.

Underwater disco, what a sight,
Oh, the jellyfish dance with delight!
In this watery world, it's quite a scene,
With bubbles and laughter, all so keen!

Midnight Caress of Water

Moonlight shimmers on the waves,
Fish in tutus, oh, how they rave!
Dolphins leap with a wink and grin,
They say, "Dancing's our favorite sin!"

Bubbles pop like confetti here,
Making music for starts to cheer.
The tide rolls in, with laughter bold,
As jellybeans swim and stories unfold.

Starfish hold a poetry night,
Reciting lines with pure delight.
Eels slip in with a funny tale,
Of tangled hair and a weak-willed sail.

The seaweed sways, a funky groove,
Octopuses join in, making moves.
Under the stars, what a comedy,
In this splashy realm, all are free!

Fluid Embrace of Twilight Tides

The tides giggle as they sneak,
Slapping the shore in a playful peek.
Sandcastles wobble, trying to stand,
While crabs declare, "This is our land!"

Seashells whisper, secrets of old,
To clams and mussels, once bold.
"Did you see that wave take a dive?
It flopped and rolled, oh my, alive!"

Seagulls wear shades, looking so cool,
As they splash down in the tidal pool.
Fish offer rides on their silver backs,
While otters slide in, avoiding the cracks.

As the sun dips low, colors burst,
Making the salty air, oh so first.
Laughter erupts, from each little fin,
In this watery world, chaos begins!

The Stillness of Salted Serenity

Seashells gossip on the shore,
About a crab who danced galore.
"Did you see him spin? What a sight!
He got dizzy, tumbled, what a fright!"

Fish decided to put on a play,
With a anglerfish lighting the way.
The starfish laughed, keeping the score,
As sea cucumbers wanted more!

Turtles in hats, doing the slow race,
While a seaweed monster hides, just in case.
The waves whisper back, in a silly tone,
"Why chase shadows when you can moan?"

Bubbles carry a funny tune,
As they drift in the glow of the moon.
In this salty world, laughter's the key,
In every splash, there's joy to see!

Echoes on the Seashore

The seagull squawks, it's quite a roar,
As tide pulls back, and sand's a floor.
A crab walks sideways, thinks it's grand,
While kids build castles, with moats so planned.

A splash! A wave, it dances near,
Tickles toes, oh what a fear!
Sandy socks are now a rage,
Playing tag with shells on stage.

The beach ball flies, with joyful cheer,
Dives and dodges, never near.
In the sun, we laugh and play,
Chasing waves, all day, hooray!

But watch your step, the tide can sneak,
And soon that crab may want to peek.
So join the dance, the silly spree,
For ocean's giggles call to thee!

Tranquil Currents Unfold

Bubbles float, like thoughts on air,
A pelican lands, with quite a flair.
Waves lap gently, a rhythmic tease,
As beach umbrellas dance with ease.

A jellyfish drifts, dressed like a gown,
While children giggle, splashing down.
The sun shines bright, a golden grin,
Don't forget the sunscreen on your skin!

Fish peek out, then dart away,
A dance of dodge, a wild ballet.
Seaweed tickles toes with glee,
Nature's joke, oh can't you see?

The tide goes in, then takes its dues,
Leaving behind some old, lost shoes.
We laugh and dance, in salty air,
Life's a bit funny, without a care!

Celestial Ballet of the Waves

Under the sun, the waves they twirl,
While starfish spin in crazy whirl.
A dolphin jumps, does flips with pride,
Making fish giggle, oh what a ride!

The surfboards glide, a comical sight,
Surfers tumble, in their best fight.
With laughter echoing, skies so blue,
The ocean winks, just for you.

Seashell messages float on by,
"Dig here!" they say, "And don't be shy!"
Mermaids giggle, splash with flair,
Winking eyes, in salty air.

As sun dips low, the day's a jest,
With crabs marching, in their best dress.
So dance along, in current's sway,
For the sea's a stage, come what may!

Gentle Swells and Silent Shores

The tide whispers secrets, soft and sweet,
While dolphins play tag, with flippers and feet.
Seashells chuckle on sun-kissed sand,
Creating moments, both funny and grand.

A kite takes flight, a comical sight,
As sea breezes tug, with all of their might.
Children run wild, leaving footprints in line,
While sandcastles tumble, that's just fine!

A clownfish sways, with color so bright,
It dodges seaweed in playful flight.
With laughter around, the waves gently roll,
Embracing the joy, with a comforting soul.

When evening falls, and the sun bows down,
The stars above wear their nightgown.
So raise a cheer for the sea's witty charms,
In its quiet dance, we find our calm.

Echoing Murmurs of the Deep Blue

Waves play tag with sandy toes,
Seagulls laugh at their great foes.
Fish wear hats, they think they're slick,
While crabs waltz, doing a quick flick.

A dolphin does a backflip, grand,
As shells cheer on, a clapping hand.
Starfish grumble, 'Why not us?'
While seaweed shakes, a colorful fuss.

Bubbles float like popcorn's burst,
Gulls dive down, they're always first.
The tide hums tunes, oh so funny,
While jellyfish jiggle, sweet as honey.

In salty air, the laughter swells,
As clowns of the sea spin their spells.
With every wave, a chuckle flows,
In this wet world, anything goes!

Beneath the Surface of Solitude

An octopus plays hide and seek,
Wearing disguises, oh so unique.
Shrimps gossip about the latest trend,
While turtles giggle, they can't pretend.

Clams whisper secrets, tight-lipped,
While fish parade, their colors whipped.
A flatfish flaps, a pancake lean,
While eels dance like they're on a screen.

Coral reefs host wild parties each night,
With sea cucumbers dancing in moonlight.
The tide's a DJ, spinning the tunes,
While snails groove beneath the blue dunes.

Lobsters sport hairstyles all askew,
As laughter echoes, bright and true.
In deep blue corners, silliness thrives,
Creatures collide, oh what a surprise!

The Still Elixir of Nature

Waves whisper secrets to distant shores,
While sea foam giggles, it never bores.
Sea urchins play poker, who's got the luck?
With shells as chips and a good old pluck.

The sun dips low, it's magic hour,
Mermaids brush hair, adorned with flowers.
Starfish juggle, putting on a show,
While winking at mussels, 'Look, I can glow!'

A pirate rock, now just a seat,
For gulls debating who tasted the treat.
Crabs in tuxedos take their grand stance,
As seaweed sways, joining the dance.

Ripples shimmer, smiles write the script,
As nature's comedy, never eclipsed.
In the stillness, laughter ignites,
Beneath the waves, joy takes flight!

Surrendered Dreams upon the Coast

Sandcastles crumble, laughs on the breeze,
As children roll, making funny knees.
A jellyfish skips, with no sense of pride,
Saying, 'Floating's the way, let's enjoy the ride!'

Flip-flops dance along beachy trails,
While seagulls plot schemes and wind-whipped tales.
Crabs tell jokes, sharing puns with flair,
As beach balls bounce, laughter fills the air.

A sand crab's high-five, too shy to land,
While sea stars plot their next bandstand.
Collecting shells, a treasure hunt's chore,
Finding laughter is the gold we adore.

With sunrise smiles, our silliness wakes,
Collecting memories in sandy flakes.
As ocean tides weave stories anew,
Surrendered dreams washing into view!

The Dance of Moonlit Waters

Bubbles pop and giggle loud,
As fish don bow ties, looking proud.
Crabs do the cha-cha on the floor,
While seahorses twirl, wanting more.

A starfish slips and does a spin,
With every flop, the crowd breaks in.
Turtles groove and take a chance,
In a swirling, snappy underwater dance.

The lighthouse shines, it's quite a sight,
Inviting waves to join the night.
But jellyfish float, with jelly in hand,
Doing a wobbly, wibbly stand!

When tide pulls back, the music fades,
As fish return to their cool charades.
The moon just chuckles, what a show!
Can't wait to see them dance, you know!

A Sway of Salt and Sand

Crabs on the shore, with buckets in tow,
Building sandcastles, all in a row.
Seagulls squawk, they're quite the crew,
Snatching snacks, just for a chew.

Waves play peek-a-boo with the land,
As surfers crash and make their stand.
Each wipeout brings a burst of cheer,
With giggles echoing far and near.

Starfish lounging, they wave goodbye,
While clams are hurting, too shy to try.
The tide rolls back, what a sight to see,
As everyone yells, "Come dance with me!"

Shells join the fun, and chirp along,
To the beat of the ocean, a splishy song.
With every sway, the world seems bright,
In a salty, sandy, silly delight!

Murmurs of the Abyss

In the depths where bubbles rise,
The squids pull faces, oh what a surprise!
Whales join with their big bass hum,
While minnows play hide and seek, feeling dumb.

Eels twist and shout, they know the groove,
Searching for friends, they wibble and move.
An octopus shows off its fancy tricks,
Doing a jig while avoiding the ticks!

The clownfish laugh, with stripes of delight,
Dancing in circles, oh, what a sight!
The abyss might seem dark and grim,
But with every wave, it's bright and brim!

In underwater caves, the games unfold,
With stories of laughter and treasures untold.
Here's to the party, where shadows reign,
A murmur of joy, without any pain!

Rhythms of the Deep Blue

The drum of the waves beats in time,
As sea turtles find their rhythm, sublime.
Dolphins leap with a roll and spin,
Making the ocean a stage to win.

A conch shell plays, a tune so sweet,
While fish dance close, in oh-so-cute feet.
Sharks try to tango, but trip on their tail,
Creating a scene that's bound to prevail!

The plankton glow, their lights they show,
As the night blooms bright with a cosmic flow.
Barnacles join in a clunky trot,
As the ocean laughs at the fun they've got!

So here's to the depths, where silliness thrives,
In a grand ballet, the ocean jives.
With every splash, a giggle to share,
In the salty embrace, we shed all despair!

Beneath the Surface

Bubbles rise like hiccups made,
Fish wear hats, a grand parade.
Seaweed sways in silly glee,
As crabs conspire for tea at three.

Jellyfish with wobbly grace,
Do a jig, a wobbly race.
Starfish play tag, on the beach,
Shells all giggle, just out of reach.

Octopus cooking a funny stew,
With a wink and a jolly hue.
Shrimps tap dance on sandy floors,
While clams debate the ocean's scores.

Coral reefs, a color show,
Fishy friends put on a glow.
Here beneath the waves, we see,
Nature's jokes, our jubilee!

Calmness Reigns

Seagulls squawk, a raucous crowd,
Waves attempt a dance, quite loud.
Each splash a chuckle, every swirl,
Even the tide has begun to whirl.

Shells gossip, oh what delight,
Sharing tales of the starry night.
Sand in my shorts, a fashion crime,
But here, I giggle; all is sublime.

Driftwood dancing, oh so bold,
Its moves are funny, quite uncontrolled.
As sea foam tickles my tired toes,
I chuckle at how the humor flows.

The sun dips low, a peachy smile,
Waves wave high, it's quite the style.
Here in the calm, so much to gain,
Life's quirks are wild; calmness reigns!

Choreography of the Dusk Tide.

As evening falls, the waves start to sway,
Doing the limbo, 'Come join the play!'
With a crash and a splash, they shuffle around,
Each wave tries to outdo the last with a sound.

Crabs in tuxedos, all dapper and neat,
Ballroom dancing, all up on their feet.
Sea cucumbers spin in a comical trance,
While dolphins join in with a synchronized prance.

The moon gives a wink, the night comes alive,
As fish leap up high, so eager to dive.
"Let's not hurry," says a wise old whale,
With a chuckle, he tells every finned tale.

As the tide twirls in its gleeful embrace,
Creatures underneath all join the race.
For under the stars, in this watery slide,
There's laughter and joy in the dusk's gentle tide.

Whispers Beneath the Waves

In the hush, there's a giggling sound,
As fish exchange jokes all around.
Clams crack up over silly puns,
While the barnacles join in for fun.

Sea turtles meet for a friendly chat,
Debating if crabs prefer hats or spat.
Anemones wave with a cheeky grin,
"Let's play hide and seek! Who'll win?"

The tide makes jokes, ebbing and flow,
Crashing along with a little show.
Whispers of laughter in watery streams,
Reveal all their secrets, like magical dreams.

As currents sway, and bubbles rise bright,
Creatures beneath dance with all their might.
In the depths where humor thrives,
Joy bubbles up, and laughter survives!

Tides in Soft Embrace

The sea hugs the shore with a gentle tease,
Tickling toes with playful ease.
Waves roll in like jokesters bold,
Bringing stories of treasures untold.

Seagulls squawk in their comical caw,
Cracking jokes with each flapping jaw.
As driftwood bobbles in a merry waltz,
Sand castles giggle, "No faults, no faults!"

Ebb and flow, a soft serenade,
As barnacles boast, "We made the grade!"
In this frothy ballet of laughs galore,
Each spray of salt brings humor ashore.

In soft embraces, the tides concede,
Every splash a chuckle, a joyful creed.
With laughter prevailing on wave's merry grace,
Nature's own jesters fill this space!

Hushed Conversations of the Coast

Gulls gossip overhead, quite the chat,
Shells whisper secrets, imagine that!
Waves tickle toes with a playful spree,
Sandcastles giggle, "Just wait for me!"

Crabs in tuxedos, scuttling with grace,
Trying to dance in a comical race.
Seagulls stealing fries, what a bold plan,
Pretending to be a sophisticated clan.

Seashells snicker beneath the bright sun,
As tides take turns in a splashy fun run!
Each droplet's a joker, making a splash,
And fish crack a joke in a bubbly flash.

With each rolling wave, a chuckle is found,
Laughter resounds in this frothy playground.
Even the breeze seems to giggle and sway,
And sunlight joins in, all sparkling and gay.

The Ballet of Water and Sand

Tiny waves prance, they leap and they bow,
While flip-flops squeak, 'We don't know how!'
The shoreline's a stage where sandcastles smile,
Waving their flags for a while, just a while!

Starfish in slippers, their dance is quite rare,
Trying to tango with the salty sea air.
A seaweed garland on a crab in a twirl,
He's the real star, making waters swirl.

Dolphins waltz high with a splash and a spin,
While scallops cheer on with a shell-tapping grin.
Barnacles boogie on rocks with great flair,
Cracking up ceaselessly—we all can't help stare!

Catch a big wave—watch it shimmy and sway,
Making artists of each seashell ballet.
Nature's own jesters, not taking a chance,
With foam in our drinks, join this festive dance!

Celestial Sighs from the Depths

Bubbles float up, like giggles from below,
Whales fashion jokes in a deep-water show.
The octopus juggles with all of its arms,
While fish in tuxedos flash all of their charms.

Starfish conferring on the best way to rise,
Flipping through currents—oh, what a surprise!
They've decided to issue a swimming decree,
That everyone should join in bubbly glee!

The mermaids are laughing, their voices like bells,
As they share sea tales and fanciful spells.
Shark in a top hat remarks with a grin,
"Dance is just swimming with a bit of spin!"

Jellyfish float by, with a wobble and sway,
"Let's have a party! Come out and play!"
As fireflies twinkle from far above head,
The dance of the deep keeps yawning instead!

Nightfall Cadence of the Waves

As dusk tumbles down, shadows take flight,
The sea's got a rhythm that feels just right.
Crickets join in with a chirp and a cheer,
While sand grains plan mischief, it's clear they're near!

Moonbeams and giggles illuminate tales,
As seashells craft stories with breezy details.
Dolphins delight in the twinkling moonlight,
Sneaking some giggles in the stillness of night.

Stars play peek-a-boo through the waves' gentle crest,
While starfish discuss who they think dances best.
The rhythm of waters, a syncopated tune,
With laughter and splashes under the moon.

Each crashing wave is a punchline it seems,
Washing away worries and all of our dreams.
As tides swish and swirl, join this nightly parade,
With laughter as echoes in nature's charade.

Ripplet Dreams in Twilight Glow

Waves crash and giggle, tickling the shore,
Seagulls on lookout, they shout for more.
Shells play hide-and-seek, in sand they lay,
While crabs put on shows, in a comical ballet.

Starfish wear sunglasses, strutting their stuff,
While jellyfish wiggle, saying 'Isn't this tough?'
Turtles glide by, all smooth and so slick,
And fish crack up jokes, as they dart and flick.

The sunset paints laughter, in hues bold and bright,
Dancing in twilight, what a fabulous sight!
Nature joins in, with a hop and a glance,
In this ripplet realm, it's a whimsical dance!

Endless giggles echo, in the balmy breeze,
As the stars come to play, with the waves and the trees.
In this watery world, where joy reigns supreme,
We'll laugh through the night, lost in a dream!

Beneath the Milky Waves

Bubbles bubble up, excited to greet,
As fish put on hats, looking oh-so-sweet.
A dolphin comes by, with a wink and a wave,
Doing flips and tricks, like it's all a rave!

Octopuses juggle, their arms in a fuss,
While shrimp huddle close, sharing tales on a bus.
Corals wear bling, a colorful type,
Making quite the scene, with their glitzy hype.

The moon sings a tune, soft and so bright,
While starry-eyed sea creatures join in the night.
In this milky world, where silliness reigns,
We dance in the water, casting off all chains!

With every splash, joy comes to replay,
As critters collide, in a light-hearted way.
All together we laugh, in this watery rave,
Beneath tides of dreams, what fun we crave!

In Harmony with the Sea's Lullaby

The waves whisper tales, of humor and glee,
As clams pull pranks, oh what a sight to see!
Starfish compete, in wiggle contests,
While silly seaweed invites them to rest.

Anemones giggle, as they shimmy and sway,
With crabs wearing shoes, what a funny display!
The inky blue squids, with their flicks and squawks,
Make everyone laugh, as they dance and talk.

Clownfish in costumes, ready for fun,
Underwater revelry, second to none!
The chorus of bubbles sing songs in delight,
We sway to the rhythm, all through the night.

With each twirl and splash, the joy starts to grow,
In this symphony of chuckles, we ebb and flow.
Together we frolic, in bubbly ballet,
In harmony we swim, through night and day!

Quiet Respite by the Briny Deep

On soft sandy beds, the sea turtles snore,
While starfish tell stories about ancient lore.
Crabby comedians, with their pinchers at play,
Make waves of laughter, in a nautical way.

Bubbles rise up, laughing beneath the tide,
With every dip and swirl, it's fun we can't hide.
Giant sea cucumbers flex with delight,
Swaying to the rhythm, what a silly sight!

In shadowy nooks, the fish have a chat,
Trading goofy jokes while dodging a cat.
The currents whisper secrets, a ticklish tease,
As we roll with laughter, moved by the breeze.

As twilight blankets the sea's laughing face,
We join in the fun, it's a glorious space.
With each crash and swish, it's clear to see,
In every wave's chuckle, there's joy to be!

www.ingramcontent.com/pod-product-compliance
Lightning Source LLC
Chambersburg PA
CBHW060138230426
43661CB00003B/469